Real Lear

Also by Claire Crowther

Stretch of Closures (2007)
The Clockwork Gift (2009)
On Narrowness (2015)
Solar Cruise (2020)
A Pair of Three (2022)
Sense & Nonsense: Essays and Interviews (ed. Carrie Etter) (2024)

Real Lear

New & Selected Poems

Claire Crowther

Shearsman Books

First published in the United Kingdom in 2024 by
Shearsman Books Ltd
PO Box 4239
Swindon
SN3 9FN

Shearsman Books Ltd Registered Office
30–31 St. James Place, Mangotsfield, Bristol BS16 9JB
(this address not for correspondence)

ISBN 978-1-84861-938-8

Poems copyright © 2007–2024 by Claire Crowther.
The right of Claire Crowther to be identified as the author of this work has been asserted by her in accordance with the Copyrights, Designs and Patents Act of 1988.
All rights reserved.

Acknowledgements

Thanks to *Bad Lilies, Blackbox Manifold, London Review of Books, Modron, Perverse, PN Review, Poetry Wales, prototype, Scintilla, Shearsman, Stand, Stride magazine, Tentacular, The Fortnightly Review, The Next Review, The North, Times Literary Supplement, Under the Radar* for publishing some of the poems in this collection.

I would like to thank the Stockwell poets (Anne Berkeley, Rhona McAdam, Sue Rose, Tamar Yoseloff) and the Helyar poets (Fiona Benson, John Clark, Julia Copus, Jane Draycott, Carrie Etter, Annie Freud, Jenny Lewis) for their regular de-stress and feedback. Linda Black, Lorna Dowell and Carrie Etter have provided friendship and support through twenty years of domination by the creative process.

Contents

STRETCH OF CLOSURES (2007)

Reconstructive Fortressing	11
Bookshelves	12
Lost Child	13
Honeymoon	14
Nudists	15
Foreigners in Lecce	16
Shine	17
City of Turns	18
Against the Evidence	19
The Sentence Mender	23
Posts	24
Motorway Bridges	26
Display on Sussex Ward	27
Cheval de Frise	28
Fennel	29
One Way System	30
Spin	31
Learner	32
Forthcoming Titles	33

THE CLOCKWORK GIFT (2009)

Petra Genetrix	37
Live Grenade	38
Once Troublesome	39
Mine Then	41
Xylotheque	42
Woman, Probably One of the Fates	43
Empire	44
The Thike	46

Wild Life of Goodbye	48
Sleeping on a Trampoline	50
Shaman Mamgu	53
Room Under the Stairs	54
Street Football	55
The Clockwork Gift	56
Outside the Beauty School	57
Ubi Sunt	58
Lucy's Light	59
A Seafront Wake for the Post-war	60

ON NARROWNESS (2015)

The Alices	63
Captured Women	64
Coincidence of Bodies	65
The Apology	66
Separation	67
Alcyone	68
Jehanne d'Arc and the Angels of Battle	69
Self-portrait as Windscreen	70
Separation Season	71
Snow at Christmas	72

SOLAR CRUISE (2020)

A Conference Dinner	75
Harvest in the Quantum Well Solar Cell	76
Foghorn	77
Short History of CERN	78
After Dinner Speaker	80
The Patroniser	81
Genia in Memoriam	82
The Ghost of Marie Curie	84

The Crystallier	85
On Not Being a Fish	87
Marriage, a Sunbeat	88
Cabin Coffin	89
Aquarius	90
Clifftop Meeting, a Flashback	91
Think Workers	92
Electricity Generation	93
Gold Standard	94
Surprise Kiss	95

A PAIR OF THREE (2022)

The Visitor	99
Physics of Coincidence	100
Mussels	101
Those Keys	102
I Ask These Questions	103
The Us	104
We Shine Love So Hard	106
Illyria by Rail	107
Moving On	108
Overheard	109
Heaven is Nothing if not Resolution	110

REAL LEAR (2024)

Lady Lear Dreams She is Young, Half-Wakes and Can't Remember	113
Is Stepping Out Dying or Being Born?	115
A Poem is a Covert Bird	116
Lear Shares her Wisdom with her Pareidolian Neighbours	117

Lear Sees Herself as Her Own Environment:
   Sward in Suburbia   119
   Cheap Street Leat   119
   Green Ceramic Stream   120
   Staircase in Frome Museum   120
Hazards and Thrown Humans   122
Crash, I Said   124
Falling from the Surface
   of the World *or* Lady Lear's Rescue   125
Ars Matria, Ars Filia   126
Lady Lear in the Canon   127
A God in Ascent   128
Panic of an Autocrat   129
Lear's Inwit   130
Word Hurt   133
Virtual Memory in Dark Matter   134
Like a Wasp Crawls On   135
Supplication in December   136
Gabbery   137
Last Supper   138
Soundsunder   140

STRETCH OF CLOSURES

Reconstructive Fortressing

They were moving about the rooms, two men.
My daughter said, I don't want to live with them.
No, I said, they will live here alone
if they buy our place. We will have gone.
Do you remember that large patch of green
I called the country? That's where we will be.

I've been wearing this flat for far too long.
It's dark though I've accessorised it in turquoise.
It works best when my skin is palest in winter.
In summer, it makes me look tacky. I am ready
to invest in a house as well-fitted as a bra.
None of that faux leopard skin, no balconettes.

How to explain this perfectly reasonable reason?
From her Juliet balcony, she squints at the Eye,
a toy Big Ben fixed, neat, inside it.
She is going to have to give up her view.

Bookshelves

Packed with who she has set out to become.
Chasing Che, Cocaine Nights, The Crone Bag.

Designing an individual at odds with Memories
of Old Dorking, a book I once gave her.

Parvana's Journey, the Crime of Father Amaro,
Koto Mama: she is in several countries

at once, probably. Meanwhile in Brixton,
that puddle left after the rain of adolescence,

her boyfriend reads The Art of Travel
while parenting her new self. Hard, I imagine.

Lost Child

Scrape the ditch that fits Hob's Moat
to Hatchford Brook. Look through oak roots,

the horse field, uphill to Elmdon.
Is she hiding behind that sky-blue Lexus?

Shout towards the airport. Planes rise
and fall as if ground were a shaking blanket.

Up there, the air hostesses smile.
Inflate your own life-jacket first.

The small original airport building stands,
apart, a mother at a school gate.

Pearl was playing quietly alone.
My ear is like a shell the wind swept.

Honeymoon

Even the rock smells its mortality,
even through millennia. Even granite
senses its exfoliation. She is

determined to see Bridal Veil Fall
but he, scared of such a steep gradient,
a cliff falling away to one side,

no fence to the path, grips any
girth, bole or boulder. Going, going,
ready or not, she shouts ahead of him.

Clouds skip flimsy dresses across
the sky. He watches out for streams, gullies,
twists his ankle tripped by swallow-holes,

stumbles over roots. Here at last
is the green lace, aqua silk,
torn, wrinkled, its slippery nature

pouring away, less like Niagara
than tears, and her, a full cast
of his own damp, uncommon faces.

Nudists

In the home of the naked, glass is queen.
A rule of sunlight on his left shoulder.
Her forearms hide a Caesarean scar

and a tied net curtain tries
to billow towards thighs that stray apart.
It serves a surprise to passers-by.

Nakedness is not the revelation
of glass. No less opaque than neighbours,
especially after dark when she loosens

the long hair of voiles. He stops talking,
notices that the window is hung with one
slant reflection of them both, framed.

Foreigners in Lecce

Home is rind-hard
so we have come here
to tarmacked marble,
angels on great walls

brought down by weather.
We look over
olive trees, whose hips tilt
above October mats,

bones and joints ready
to shake down the little
fruit they carry. An outburst
of autumn birds, like rust

or falling oranges
in a courtyard. Now
something asleep in us
is blown like glass.

Shine

A plasticised fabric cover on a motorbike,
petrol blue and green of peeling eucalyptus trunk,
the still water in a granite bowl in a calmly
horizontal driveway: all hang with shine.
Imagine
its subtlety, even inside my muscle where streams
of glycogen gleam as climbing dams them for sugar.
We play shine – we swap
glazed posters of Culture Clash and Rawson Democrat,
wheelie bins for calla lilies.
Now our shine,
like lesser stars, has darkened, we can identify
better, things that shine, vitreous, resinous, splendent,
anything adamantine – cars like water droplets
splashed on the hot bypass, boats like tiny stones skimming
the marina, spots of tarmac lustre.
Think of us
next to these images, retinues of the sun,
as salts of silver, bromide or chloride, blackening
in light. We pause, absorbed by garden rooms, their retinas.

City of Turns

The sea rolled itself into a sweat
down our faces as if the tide
had suddenly thought of us as inlets

while radiant-crested, gorgeously-winged
dark-red and orange container crates
trembled from cranes on the dock

and a dead foal's eyes stared toward them
along a horizon striped with steel.
Ripples of sand spread to her mane

relaxed as if from running. The dunes
hid other burials. I covered
the head with my shirt. My breasts,

salt quartz. Seagulls curfewed
an eagle. A shovel of wings packed him off
across this city of turns, the sea.

Against the Evidence

I like jostle. You and I a crowd.
Aggregate in the station yard.
In the carriage, arms along an ear,
thigh pressed to a baby's head,
Friday breath through the gap of faces.

A woman wearing long black velvet
glides through our carriage, flies the carpet
that locks feet. Arcs of air open
in front of this ghost and close behind,
fading passengers out. They don't realise.

Deva, I thought, or dea abscondita,
when she began to hang across my light,
a jalousie. It was the night you stayed.
Since then, Piera has arrived and gone
with you but speaks only to me.

I get up every morning, convinced
we'll live forever, against the evidence,
and call that happiness. I think of scientists
researching the expansion which will be
the end of our universe, not just my world,

who will recall, like that end, all ghosts
including her. But lately, she has shown
you are equally ghost in my life, the lover
without rights, appearing on my pavement,
on my flight, in my albergo.

Your hands among my papers established
their own directions and hours, as lawless
as Piera is. You have both researched me
and I shall track her down, my bracket of lies.
She skates all the way to Porto Badisco

and leaves us there for an hour alone,
and alone on the fleur de lis
of the hotel bedspread, mocking me
for chasing her living self yet pushing
her ghost into the drawer with the Gideon bible.

Saturday. Lemon of winter. Damp charcoal
bramble. Grey quilts of cloud. Wind tumbles
the wrapping from our ciabatta as if *future*
is the rim of a beaten country
and we've reached it. I want the ghosts

in every word to stand too close
to wheel-splash as Piera does,
to stalk low bridges like double-deckers.
We shrink, one surface after another,
flesh then soil, marble then Lecce tufa,

the local stone made of giant fossils.
Piera used it. Her work dissolved
as if it were the custard Dentoni,
the Big Teeth, moulded for crema.
Fourteen-eighty. Snow.

That cold Friday, she carved
a Passion. A down of limestone
and holm-oak fell from her adze.
Wild peacock meat screamed in the pan.
The Adriatic tore itself like veiling.

Piera thought of ground diamond,
the finest known poison. A husband's hand
smells like tufa, warm, rough,
open to the weather. She walked from town,
wearing the mail shirt he had forgotten,

to find the wet eyes of rock.
The storm tore holes in bark,
picked off boulders, ripped up frail
olive mats, plucked at boar bristle.
The soles of her shoes shouted, control us.

To find the hidden cave, his discovery,
his place to take women. Slippery.
They would clutch him while the sea spat
balls of white saliva at a cliff
that let its strata go like leaves.

Piera haunts any hint of pleasure:
the subterranean nymphaea, the bars,
stone fences where the horses waited,
the busty saints bulging from church roofs,
jacuzzi bath, neon logo pouring

apple brandy. They decay
into an abandoned industrial area
when Piera joins us. You don't see her.
You insist I imagine blacked-out windows,
broken-boned blinds, wisps of plastic.

I didn't arrange to meet a ghost,
yet there she was, in the British Library,
at Waterloo, in Caffè Nero,
watching our affair. We were her map
from that first rush-hour you pushed through

to say I was your genius, to say thanks,
to tell me dates and times I had appeared,
a sign to you that life would work again.
She had been a footnote in the book
I was writing on Puglian nymphaea.

It was you who called her out of her paper
shroud, up from my bibliography,
when you called me. Today, we drift
through Lecce alleyways, their marble sills,
past men with hair the colour of hot tarmac,

and faces that are redrafts of Caravaggio,
posters of Berlusconi out of Caesar.
She sips every glass of red you drink.
You don't even notice the mouth print.
Sunday evening. You'll go home alone.

When soft Lecce stone is cut,
the guide says, *in loro passa virtute,*
che le pregia, e che l'indura:
virtue enriches it and hardens it.
She murdered them, husband, mistress,

hauled the big rocks to fill
the natural gateway to the cave
where, she shouted to the wind, no-one
was laughing at the weather, wrapped
in down, hot as the smell of drying canvas.

Fragments of her art are buried in crypts,
her scarlets, purples. We are history.
But non-existence poses a singularity.
The end of passion is counter-intuitive.

The Sentence Mender

I carry my voice out at night away from our house to West Hill junction.

There is a seat by the bus stop. Drivers pull in, in case I want to board.

I wait

alongside engines and sirens

till heels, brakes, horns, cut-off exhausts, the blue hat man, phones, wheels

have quietened,

till black sacks have been shredded by foxes and strewn at my feet and maple leaves have diminished to bronze stars on the paving stones.

Then I storm this firmament,

blare from scaffolding, against murders of windows, in the drizzle of twenty-four hour supermarkets.

At home, my husband hates the sound of me.

I work on it in the garage,

a sentence-mender.

Posts

i
gateless gateposts extruded
out of frontage going home
my friend C who has had a
lump biopsied needs to be
surprised by an odd though
comfortable topic to make a
turn from our uptight necks

ii
look there she says the sunny certainty
of that Cotswold stone untopped broad
footed post the word lodge carved
in Victorian letters it's
been there for over a
century the left post's
gone and a sweep of
drive the house violet
wild buddleia strokes its limbless shoulder

iii
unemployed gateposts stand
at the eleven storey flats and
Park View nursing home the
millionaire's house unfenced
council estates we park there
C climbs out quietly her body
nibbled only by men sons Dr
husband he waves from their
folly built in the thirties like a
pleasure dome rain and sun
dissect the brick a bare front
garden no grass gravelled to
two cars' width an iron portal
lettered PALACE in an echo
of pre-war wit welcomes her
to the private future of a lost

iv
domain
her home's
graceful posts
are bluish veined
delivering territory easily
through a landscape of past
values they're round she said
I've never noticed my round
gateposts repointed so
often by my husband
no gate in our time

Motorway Bridges

The seven a.m. news chips in and out.
A cannibal on trial. The two women
killed each week by partners are designated
a government priority. My body

is similar to how it was before
the diagnosis was made but there are words
now. The announcer is muffled by each bridge.
My wipers stick on light rain. I've tried

to glimpse my fate in the wing mirror … not telling
anyone. Morning unwraps a bolt
of hedge in dark lengths. Milošević can't
attend a judgment on genocide. I'd opt

out of treatment on any grounds – the nurse
holds my flinches in case I spill the chemical.
A word I'm thinking of is (irrelevant) 'henge'
because fogged concrete looks like stone.

Display on Sussex Ward

Yarrow: verdant, ravelled yarnburst,
shells of thread
cloud the emerald hills
of Vandyke and double featherstitch,
whipped web and long-armed feather.

I reach out. A man points to a notice:
'Don't touch.'
The paper gown, hung up
like art in this cubicle, will be creased
by the patient clutching pants and shoes.

Cheval de Frise

It was because she wasn't overlooked
because our street is one-side only
and opposite the full length of our houses
there's a wall, it's because no view,
that my neighbour hung a balcony
across her upper storey. The first

stand-out. They multiplied, a gallery
to step onto, raising knees high
through windows and through French doors.
They float us in the air like life jackets
but, even so, we grip the canvas scaffold
of deckchairs when we set down mugs

on armrests, balance sunglasses
on the rims of flower pots, in order
to stare at lichens, mosses, water stains
and those ancient regular naked boles
of parasite, we've learned, an *epiphyte*
that escalades over the coping, invisibly

leaving behind the glass and iron spikes.
Our mews is mentioned in the Area Guide
so tourists occasionally come to see
'*the cagey prominences*'. But for us,
whoever owns it, whatsoever it blinds –
grass pissing seeds inside dumped factories,

elder saplings cracking through concrete,
limbless petrol pumps, padlocked shafts –
however chafed with particulates,
it is that bent-shouldered, standing wall
that makes our heritage. What blank thing
do you look at without altering?

Fennel

Zesting all over my front garden, how her fennel clings
to the removal men. As if it is interested
in boxes. In my leaving today. I haven't trimmed it.
It fixes on my shoulder. Neither have I named this house,
this semi, as she begged me to, Fennel Cottage.
The new owners may scrape the taste of my house
off its surface, but her fennel seeds cranny in fissures
and plan a dynasty of yellow tang.

Spin

The window dresser forgets bodies, steels pleats, pins cloth, a charcoal that ticks with blue and red, gathers softness in a stiff weave as if he were voiding grey sky of cloud to make draperies that could float inside basilica domes.

He poises stuff in movements Gap and Next ignore.

Above him, a sign: shears open,

points up. Who reads his window? In the absence

of graphics and words, models and ready-mades, we still see the shapes of men, kicked, spun, a regiment of uncut rolls tumbling onto a battlefield, unmeasured.

Along this stretch of closures, his window is lit.

Mail hangs in adjacent doors.

Like Christmas, the mall is coming.

One-way System

In a landscape of spectacular wrappers,
huge electric adverts promise transport
beyond Capitol Studios, Ace Wine,
the marble and slate yard, and a man
stooped, unshaven, grey hair, stands

at the bus-stop – an advert for a passenger,
full of expectation – as if the bus,
parked, empty of a driver, is ready
to move to the boarding point, open
its doors, take us. We hang back.

We don't assume the 77A
will recognise its queue, won't smile
towards it but face the Huguenot houses,
restored refugees. They are solicitors'
offices, now, a listed Site of Hope.

Learner

We used to hear him practise all the time,
midwifery of music. Two men
grappled the bulk of his piano down
three flights. Wooden veneer splintered.

To me.
Back.
Tricky.
Bit of a corner.
Easy.
Easy.
Hold it.
Nicely.
Now.

There was a bumping down of delicate sounds.
A delivery of loss out of rehearsal.

Forthcoming Titles

untitled
words selected randomly each day from an original brief to create
a wall-hung definition of death
Titled:
Definition of Death

untitled
medical plates of the dead brain collected from assorted hospital
archives
Titled:
Dead Head Shots, Interior

untitled
plaster casts of family and neighbours in appropriate shades hung as
domestic decorations. Marie has her eyes open
Titled:
Short Cuts

untitled
photographic studies of flesh lit to illuminate death blows
Titled:
Shiners

untitled
technologically inspired sadomasochistic fetishes which have been
implicated in a death, each with linked tabloid headline
Titled:
Thumbscrew to Palmtop

untitled
constant-play video recording of the artist in conversation,
constructed wholly of phrases used by dying celebrities with an
unnamed friend

Titled:
I Shall Make an Attempt to Fill the Void

THE CLOCKWORK GIFT

Petra Genetrix

I won't replace lost wedding cutlery,
its broad straight limbs,
with new shallow spoons,
their writhing shoulderless handles—

Lines get broken.
All I see in museums
is the frozen watchfulness of a previous home.
Ancient knives found under Eden Walk are flints

polished in an age defined by how it ate.
There's no matching greenstone and dolomite
though I could still buy old patterns,
shell, feather, rat tail.

'Granny, did you throw away your silver?'
'The table of the moon is laid with it.'

Live Grenade in Sack of Potatoes Story

The schizoid boy who never takes his pills
and has been ordered not to visit any female
family member, here he comes, half-naked,
down to my basement. Later, a police dog bites
his scrotum. I buy chips and biscuits. Mutter
names. I take care of these grandchildren.
Like that unfed, sleepless child – the number
of games I thought up, but she's live, a grenade,
buried and ready to explode, dug up
decades after the war, lost in a sack
of potatoes. They come for my expertise.
It's worth their battering the door
to share my anger. *Nonna, oma, nain.*

Once Troublesome

'Let them call her a wicked old woman! she knew she was no such thing.'
Vita Sackville-West, *All Passion Spent*

It isn't New Year yet so Happy *What?*
Till then, it's Boxing Day every morning.
Empty bags hang off the radiators.
Chilly: hot
        cold
                Cordelia position.
      Did it mean
we didn't love each other
that morning he gave me up
though that same night he said let's marry?
    My striped dress hung
              along my body
                      bounced
              boldened
          bitmapped
my abdomen as I walked, a balloon
           sinking back down
           its own string
       after the decision.
The baby would have had to sleep in a drawer.
              Immortalists
(not you who refuse to believe improbable notions)
think:
    the smallest cell refuses to die
      in its everness.
Now I live in an attic
garden is the chewed melon skin of sky.
Old bins, old books. Death's hardly ethical
in the light of such continuity. Last week,
the CEO of a charity named in my will
wrote to suggest ways to retrieve what I've lost.

Look, Christmas photos
       of others' other
              children. After
                      Pocoyo, Juggling Balls.

Mine, Then

for those grandmothers who parent AIDS orphans

We sat on the bench outside the clinic
and I explained that they might need medicine.

I said, 'There is weather coming,
full of variety.

Wouldn't you like an umbrella
if it rains?' On the way home

it was as easy to make them laugh
as to find a vein.

I could see straight through that mousey light
to evening,

past houses pale
as my own finger,

across the pewter surface of salted road
edged by leafless trees.

The ground heaved
with sealed-in bluebells.

They worried I would be less upset
than when my own child died.

You need one person to be loved by
like a lightning flash needs dousing in a peach cloud.

Xylotheque

My husband mocks the ghost who hovers near me
on walks. A ghost wouldn't climb a stile
or skirt cows so widely. And why would she edge
round barely flooded fields? Leaky shoes?

Aren't ghosts violent, my husband suggests.
No, you need a body for that, to be
as well as mean and seem, though the ghost wears
blue jeans, sequinned boots and says

she was bullied for being beautiful
as a teenager and loved a mechanic
from Dollis Hill at twenty. The ghost noticed me
in the doctor's surgery. I held

a child who snuffled my hand like an animal.
Dying is being born. You imprint on the person
you see last. I remember her panic.
Receptionists corralled the waiting room.

Calling her up now seems like human-stealing.
My husband mocks: 'You saw a death. Why
exaggerate?' Maybe because, without ghosts,
we are a wooden library, books about wood

bound in wood with leaves for pages, words,
the seeds and nuts of ancient beech, birch, oak
and rowan. I look for her where
box trees curl like knots of neglected hair.

Woman, Probably One of the Fates

> *'This is one of a number of representations of hideously ugly old women by the same hand...'*
> Exhibit note, National Gallery of Scotland, Edinburgh

When wrinkles etch so deeply they lattice neck
and muzzle forehead, skin takes over,

makes a fabric of old stone. What I see
in my inner arm when it's bare and bent, raising a glass,

is Fate holding her drapery. It's what I expect
though bones would be more likely. Here is an outstanding
                breastbone.

And veins tunnel out the hand. While marble grabs its opportunity
to empty sockets of eyes and teeth – skin is resistance.

Empire

It was all Latin to us
      the way the box hedge
            tore through a white dress
of *convolvulus arvensis*.
Buxus sempervivens.
      We looked the lot up
           in a coffee table book
Familiar Wild Flowers.
Toad flax and poppy
      went for a strategy
           of abundance that year
we moved in
but only watercoloured
      the tough old box.
             The successful cohabitees,
in the end, were drab,
dressed with London cool.
      Ajuga reptans,
           named by Pliny
for its power to drive away
who knows what,
      cowered, bore
           only seven or eight
flowers to the head.
Other labiates,
      deadnettle and betony
           and the supposedly graceful
Festuca elatior,
cramped under wicker fingers
      that could slit hands,
           your eyes once.
You tried to dig it out.
Its roots are infected

      by some virus
                that turns the clay soil
round the stems to cement.
The tiny eyes of its leaves
        flash open each year
                among dog grass,
dog campion, dog roses.

The Thike

Here in Hob's Moat we know
a thike is not a species of devil
but, unhappily, receives attention.

A mammal, the small-lifed thike,
flourishes in our dry moat
among those buried outside graveyards.

Ranked first of unknown fauna,
a thike is easily seen from the A road,
fooling near its wood. The number of thikes

casually shot is high.
Celebrities on Channel Five News
have endorsed the policing of thike-baiters.

The community is stunned. The prevalence
of a unique English animal
is like a local murder. A primary teacher,

our most famous resident, author
of ninety books, has lectured to us often.
He says we have been thinking like Australians.

Ask instead what factors influence
the occurrence of a moated society.
No doubt our thikes begin to feel extinct.

But the mood of Hob's Moatians is hopeful
while ThikeSafe Company men,
wearing white, squat on concrete in garages,

open plastic lunch boxes and release
the thikes they have secured with nothing more
than broken clothes hangers. Remember,

when you hear a Fastruk lorry
reverse, screeching, thikes lack ears.
We elect the animals we harbour.

The Wild Life of Goodbye

I worked out how thikes talked, by touch.
They combed that butter-coloured fur with a long revv up
each strand, measuring distance from the head, pulling or pushing.

                    They gave each other permission to
                    touch—the neck, underbelly—and spoke
                    fast. Linguists charted their range of
                    sounds; semantics, no.

I learned to hear them say, *Come back to the hollow.*
Heard their names. I have no idea, being a poet,
whether they lived in peace or in violence like their end.

                    That older female by the traffic island,
                    hair flattened—how the rush hour traffic
                    rubber-necked to see her, a thike out of
                    her moat. That mass of blackening yellow
                    on the *News*.

The cullers left the feet alone. Thike's feet
stick to any surface, their soles a suction-pad
beneath boneless muscle. The carcasses
smell of fresh grouting.

It was hot but I didn't notice how short of breath
the sky, how a summer lung can't speak
without breaking. From my eyrie above
the *Medieval Fayre*, no homogeny to hair,
hair holds no hegemony for crowns.

> Everyone is feral, a deer counts notes, a dog tugs a child's paw with hands like teeth. In Hob's Moat today, an ill pale yolk of sun. Pheasants dashed into the wood. The male watched the female dip her head in steaming clay.

The grass! It's lost its tread. Cruising thunder makes breeze panic. Against the window, my arms are strips of silver, run moon solder.

Sleeping on a Trampoline

I find her sleeping on our large tramp,
neatly in the middle. Heels on the metal
springs. A human thike.

A child buzzes in my head, trapped.
Usually a child takes my hand and up, whee,
a few moments, then brings me down, my feet

plunge into sturdy skin, the palm throws me
back at a long day's sky like a duck, shuttlecock,
bee, the smack of body against my bones,

not-hug, not-massage, not-relax-you're-cared-for,
only a continent moving by my right shoulder.
Breathing, not jumping: I watch her till she wakes,

the human thike. Silent, though this one talks
for hours. 'When I was born, I was so desperate
to get out, I called to a passing neighbour,

from the uterus. She told my mother
I was about to jump. You never hear the word
outside Surrey. You're thikey, not a woman,

not a man. A night timer. There's always
someone who saw the thike in the woods at night
or sitting in the square at three a.m.

You never ask, what were *you* doing
out, spying on the thike in the small hours.
There isn't any therapy for thikes,

only for hate crimes. Other villages
make saints, celebrities. Ours makes thikes.
I don't have to accept this? And you're a woman?'

It's not because I'm dirty
It's not because I'm clean
It's not because I kissed a thike
inside a space machine

It was a common word once. Pepys' diary,
earliest known mention, bar mummers' plays:
Home where the thike is come out of the country.

Keats' letter: *I think upon crutches like the thikes*
in your Pump Room. Matthew Arnold, a rare
attempt at definition: *Thikes were boys*

whose good character was easily regressed.
Monk Lewis: *She wasn't conversational. Whether shy*
or as a result of her theikism, no one could tell.

I ask what I should call her. 'Say hello
fartface, for all I care.' Our new estate
is carefully designed not to be repetitive.

That's why we moved back to the village from town.
(Not strangers. Remember the summerhouse factory?
We've got a memento, the old sign: SOUND

YOUR HOOTER at 5 MPH.) Paint flakes off the words.
Some large houses, some small, irregular roofs,
red, green, grey tiles, a pond to fulfil

the quality of life clause. Nobody said
there were still thikes. Grasshopper baby,
she's shivering. I can tuck her in again,

cover her with spit. Or jump till dawn.
Bouncing is resisting repetition, not
enduring it. My feet slip on news

paper covering the tramp, layers starting
to compost, a thick cold grey pudding, marbleised
with black streaks. A black rim lines each frame

of sky as if glass draws away from wood.
Whee. Up a string of path, spun from the machine
of height to its overhang, its large mouth.

I reach my hand into sorbet, crystalline height,
whipped up business. She is only a crescent moon
of shoulder. The village job that nobody does.

We lean into the machine. The magnifying
glass of dark shows me what I've missed,
pushes past my artefacts, leaving them heaving.

Gradual grey smears round clouds and fists
of treetops. A hiccough of birds. Like going up
to bed, stairs set into the wall,

a chimney into rock, so steep. It's a mistake
to come back down again. You'll be damaged
by blacked out windows, masked eyes, silence,

locked doors. It makes you agree to wrong
ideas even at slow speeds unless
someone warns you first, sounding the hooter.

Shaman Mamgu

It is a shadowy night-like light today; car after car,
shiny but sepia. But look at us!
We aren't hueless! Tiny pedestrians scampering
in between lorries, white wisps of a granddaughter's hair
against my hennaed Afro, her blanched hand clasping
my red-nailed thumb. The sounds are of day—ambulance whining
down a No Entry with full spectrum Doppler effect while nose
after nose of plane parts the cloudbank, ready for Heathrow.

And our actions have been anything but pallid: an old woman scolding
the police who held a child. Her arms flicker. An officer
turns the flat of his hands toward her, berating air.
Between grey-hooded girl and red hair, our staring
is so healthy it could cure break-bone fever.
Lorries at an amber light talk in gravelly voices,
unbrick, rebrick this dark afternoon.

Room Under the Stairs

Crushed against stair rises, no
    pushing the hard margins apart
        but I tried to lounge, one foot
            buried in a flank of brushed cotton,

a lost bale. Outside, on the stairs,
    my mother's feet, stubby substitutes
        for words. My grandmother's steps
            breathed in-out-in to the top.

Dark books hunched like handles
    of cases in the nearly midnight
        in there. Every folded muscle
            ached. Upside bones were crazed

with needles. Air, packed with scales
    from unfinished wall, struggled into my lungs.
        I was filling two tins and closing
            smiling dog lids when my mother slid

across red tiles into the light
    rule around the door. We went shopping.
        Who can say
            why I had to collapse my imagination?

Street Football

You could hear new tines of glass, let out like children,
stick the wind. Then the Shrove ball flew above

the greensand caves, yells drumming it north past
the Brewery and the Dust Destructor. It landed on

a drunk, shaking a collecting tin. Back from alleys,
yards and windows, up, up until it staggered

toward Turner, Sauberge—where my mended kettle
was ready on Ash Wednesday—the ball bounced off

the diapers of Chitty's brickwork, sprinkled Nanny Puttock
from her fountain—come in, boys, she beckoned—soared

as far as Pump Corner, brushed black suits hung
along Fielders' window. Tall Percy palmed the last

drop of rain. Because my hands had practised taking
Matchpeller's dog when it sprang, my bones were fit to break

to confiscate the ball and—flash—no-one stopped
a grandmother catch, a game finish. Men boiled over

Master Woodger's muffins. Fattened, Gaffer Boult,
dressed as Grandma Wolf, stood up on gouty feet.

The Clockwork Gift

Behind the glass in Burgerzoo, fingers probed
bark. Elongated aye-aye fingers.
Larvae hid in hollows.

A tape of crickets over Blur. My granddaughter
opened a Kid's Bag. I wound
the clockwork gift.

Her legs were striped with shades of pink wool.
When did I think
of wearing black and grey?

She'd been dispensed by her mother with rose
skirt, coat. The aye-aye was tethered
to a tree trunk by its tail

twice body length. 'What's an omen of evil?
Why can't an aye-aye go home?'
A naked ear turned right, left.

Outside the Beauty School

Twilight Hour for Senior Customers.
The trees turn, in a May
that pulls their branches gently inside out,
and paints charcoal bark with green polish.

While trees think they're not trunk-stopped
on one spot, it is as good a season as any
for wings to pulse, swollen reddish-pink;
for a heart to rise to it, float up and beat in the wind.

Ubi Sunt

Where are they now, the transparent walkways,
office to office, tear-shaped desks,
the turning necks of chairs, head rests?

Sand blows through the levels. At night,
the corners are penetrated with floodlight.
The high cheekbones of the Place du Dôme,

the Comfort Hotel, glint. Bodies move
like smoke on granite mirrors. Not my storey;
that's empty, panes broken, its eery

insides deny I ever started there,
young, skipping up the run of stair;
deny I worked my whole life behind glass.

Lucy's Light

The rain is slipping them out of their ceremonies
to begin winter, her father walking the garden
threatening to cut down the bare plum
and pear, and her mother running
after, pleading that the trees
will fruit next summer,
grandmother's hurta
eaten together while they ask
the longest moon to scatter silver in
their hair at an angle so narrow that each
sees the bits of blackened iron stuck in grass
at their feet as cloves in the shining flesh of apple.

A Seafront Wake for the Postwar

The ruin on the island keeps away: fragmented steps,
shoulder bone of upper storey arch, lady chapel, rank
of skinned arms cracked at the wrists.

New houses creep near like animals listening to the old—
Teach Me Tonight—magnified through a trumpet
fixed to the mother-board.

My time was blonde scraped up in a froth. Now our white hair
is arranged against purple. From birth, the agenda of regeneration
confuses us. 'Skip it.'

I read future time by Attlee as surely as if those clock hands, beamed
on the wake wall from a light disguised as a camera, are snapping
facts. All of it is skin

though now it shakes loose of flesh, once stock still like rock inside.
An old man's hands flick his horsetail metres.
The wind turbines rush round.

'Pat's been a Samaritan since July.' 'My new man has a boat.'
Sea gatefolds each page of wave and tears.
The Struggle is Over.

ON NARROWNESS

The Alices

I said he was brillig and I meant it.
He stood in the hall of a friend's house
offering extra as simply as a hostess
carrying crockery, the only one of us

who has actually fought the jabberwock,
whose face we see on News at Ten,
whose name is called at tribunals, who defies
James Naughtie on Today. He talked

about mome raths, saying hesitantly,
'If the raths don't outgrabe.'
I loathed seeing him like that, stooping
below somebody's lintel, being slithy.

'It's not about gyring,' he snapped.
But it was. Later he told me how
after a tough meeting, in the distance
he'd seen me climbing out of a car,

my flesh suggesting something else to save.
The houses our set restored fetch fortunes.
Is that better behaviour? A brillig affair!
So special a person to have taken to wabe.

I thought, they all do it, the toves.
The tension, the criticism they get
for neglecting their children, the fear
of borogoves. We support them,

us Alices. But we're mome. 'To me
you could never be mome,' he said
'whatever you decide,' as he left.

Captured Women

And in that house there was a room
That was hung with many drawings
Of women with their mouths tight
Shut, lips making a point:
'Why do you stand in front of us?
Why stand there? Why not go?'

One dipped her curls forward
Thoughtfully: 'Why don't you hang?
When will you go?' Their hair, serious
Expansion of each, upwards, sideways,
A boundary against the questions:
'Why are we on the brink of you?'

The pencil asked what hair weighs
And drew it to cover the tucked-away
Technology of ear. Listen.
The captured women ask: 'Why
Do we hang in front of you?
Why hang here? Why don't we go?'

The jib of them, their hissing sound
Like woodpeckers or worried finches
Considering a swing at the seeds
Before flight from the sparrowhawk:
'Why do we hang here while you stand?
Why don't we go? Why don't we go?'

Coincidence Of Bodies
for Beatrice Tinsley, astronomer, 1941–81

The heavier I was, the more I shaped space
round me. Mass curves space. Come on eclipses, you never
could have blocked me. I curved new space.

But my own flesh was moon. It eclipsed
the larger body of sun in the coincidence of distance
that makes them equal, that allows

measurement of the bend of stars.
I was flesh. Had I been only that mass coordinating
old allegories that must be Love

or Sensuality, I would have appealed
for the fleshlessness I have now, I'd have begged not to be
a monument of blood.

And if I'd survived till fallen flesh
changed my shape so it wasn't hunted or held up, would I
have resolved the paradox of flesh –

that I was made of more than I am?
Mars, you wore only a helmet half off to show us flesh
is too frail for battle. My fabric now

is lighter than flesh, the blue of galaxies.
I am what has been proved of the coincidence of bodies,
given I'm not short-lived and can eclipse.

The Apology

Mosquitoes charged me with their sour sugar
outside the vinegar house. Six years, ten years,
sixty, it ferments from oak to juniper
to chestnut to cherry and back to oak wood barrels,
balsamic vinegar separating itself
from a hundred year old mother sediment.

Breathe in through the unstoppered hole.
Smell it changing. This is immortality
but that sweet vinegar didn't comfort my ill friend.
She hovered towards my slight sore throat.
I shouldn't have let her low immunity near me.
My virus would order us differently,

her life for one ciao, and down she goes
to that atomic level, eternal future,
for which our short lengthening time ferments us.
Next day I said to my body
(my body thinks my voice is God):
'You handle poison too well.

Your itch denies my taste for eternity,
it's anciently made.' Then my body says,
'I'm giving you time.' So I called to say sorry.

Separation

Snails might shout
crawling from mint to balm 'I burn'
or call from lovage and hosta

'I'm burning dry'
while my husband is falling asleep
in the sun away by Muker Beck,

where oyster catchers
freeze on their nests and only water stays
awake, irritably controlled, pushing

stones, stuck, stuck, stuck, stuck, till we both are
woken by pain with its orange beak.

Alcyone

On an unfenced cliff, frightened
at the edge, in a million
silverfish of rain, I found

my sister Alcyone.
To me, it was just sand
crowning, a bitten earth

on which silt has built
for eight thousand years, an inch
a month. Still builds. She listened

to gulls whittle the neediness
of quiet. She watched a ship
slip into pearl while sunset

picked up importance. Look,
how brown bracken squats,
prickles with fragility

under squalls that dig into
the shoulder muscles of gusts. Gusts
that coil and bounce beyond all

elastic limit. Young winds.
Young winds I think like you.
I'm not over that hour,

Jehanne d'Arc and the Angels of Battle

They were carrying elaborate armour, when they broke in,
to lock me in.

This metal face,
these sleeves can't be undone. I think I'll suffocate. This hard face

is so heavy that, in itself, it could kill. I pitied them
when I saw them;

since they flew off
I haven't always been believed in, myself. First they took off

great muscular structures from their shoulders. Those wings were steel.
Put me in steel,

I said. I was
not touched otherwise except to hear words ransack me. Word was,

soldiers pray to me as if I am what was brought of value.
What I value

inside metal
is, my galvanised skin thinks it's dominant. Helpless metal.

Self-Portrait as Windscreen

Do you think I'm clear on every issue
just because I'm glass?
Have you heard yourself calling 'Claire,

Claire, Claire, Claire' when you're confused?
A name is lulling
when you aren't clear on every issue.

So your favourite phrase 'Let's be clear
on this one thing'
is the public face of 'Claire. Claire.'

I see you everywhere, using my nature,
hardened from soft,
imagining you're clear. Fired, made

to soften, harden again. We're laminated.
The crack that comes
won't shatter us or your calling.

Separation Season

Cold bamboo
was hatching, cross-hatching; dead
stem arches

aisled the field. Tractors decayed
at the edge.
Drivers had thrown to rot what

will not rot.
Our plan had wintered. Though
branches milled

their twigs to silver, still ice
crawled away
from what it had taken on

and the sun
stopped chasing mist to wire
and rays woke

mistletoe to emerald
on the oak.
Our jewels had nested here.

Diamonds,
opals begged *don't repeat us
dissolve us.*

Move, I said, now you can move.
Fissured field,
frozen for months, you've rested.

Snow at Christmas

I've thought of snow as a raptor that seizes
holly,
ivy, all the evergreens, a dog that bites
a child
near the eye. It turns to dirt. I'm used to trees
that rear
and don't lean towards me or bow down like this.
I stopped
to sense temporal and carotid points of
welcome
and the snow ushered me into the garden's
charge, pink
sky packaged as a giant jay's breast, puffy
and shy
on a witch hazel. We haven't read a word
since then
all Christmas but proper names, prepositions
and love.

SOLAR CRUISE

A Conference Dinner Takes the Future on Board
– in my view

Once-powerful dock. Historic boat:
the *S.S. Eschatology*.
Sweet talk, run softly till the feast is over.
> *– meet the particle physicists,*
> *funded for findings in *Rapture Physics, and*
> *waiting out the End Times, defining small*
> *matter. The marvels of nano-beginnings,*
> *debris of the first particle, gleam and go in*
> *the shy firefly Higgs boson.*

So when an old solar physicist
stands up, in shrunken jeans, sandals,
and says, 'All we need are extravert bosons,

streams of golden photons that will free
new current. Leave the Higgs to hide…'
> *– of course, there is no applause.*
> *Sir Olkincole shakes a corporate, corporeal*
> *hand among the suits.*

But my old physicist's emerald forest flourishes:

crystal-quick cells, experimental
leaves, threatened species. If one bee
should soar to swarm and undulate and carry

time to change … one student stands. She claps.
She barefaces fuss.

> *Future: you brim with data for us.*

Harvest in the Quantum Well Solar Cell Reminds Me of Lipstick

'Look,' my physicist says. I look.

There: a speck of disc
in his palm. 'Cheaper
cleaner fuel. No
more nuclear waste.

Red Hazard

No more stink of oil

Cursed Purple

with this crystal: gall-
ium arsenide
quantum well solar cell:

I keep it on me.
Here,' he says. I hear:

Sunstalkin

Foghorn with Solar Harvester

Beneath and around his palm
on which balances one possible future
the Atlantic
calms
and swells.
                A sheen of fog curtains our balcony
                and into that the captain sends a throaty

                          ohhhhm

                          ohhhhm

                          ohhhhm

A Short History of CERN* by Two Physicists

i A Particle Chaser's Soliloquy

Why am I here?
To build an upside down duomo.

To shaft through Jura rock.
>*On Lowering Day, someone dropped a spanner.*
>*It missed tons of sinking machinery.*

To command a yard of copper wire
down here among the orange hard hats.

To monitor the silver pipe. It beams
protons that smash themselves and make
new particles.
    A nanosecond later,
another crash, more bunches of new beings.

To find which particle is which.
To hunt the Higgs boson through beam-born bits,
as many people as live in North America.
>*It's so short-lived, it's never been seen live.*

To saddle sunlight,

to smack the flanks of photons and send up
data to where a thousand computers stare
down through their sweating floor to the pantheon.
To name what's been particularised.
>*Why, how light a thing a boson can be:*
>*a weightless waving string of photons,*

> *that hit our retinas, wake us*
> *to the multiplicity we call nothing.*
> *There they play, bosons of zero mass*
> *while Higgs lurks, heavy, invisible.*

To tell its resurrection,
to do so together.

ii The Rarest Particle

My physicist left CERN halfway through his career. There would be no more researching the world's first moments as a high priest of Rapture Physics once, on CERN's preprint library shelves, he'd found David Mathisen's 1979 thought experiment testing the world's last moments.

Not that a Rapture denier might not share some qualities with a Rapturist: vision, dedication, a conviction that he has theorised the Truth and only needs to get it into service. The Professor, my experimental physicist, is a natural Rapturist. The difference is that his rapture will be the gathering up of humans into the mortal future of the earth rather than their gathering up into the immortal extinction of their species.

One hundred years to the day that Einstein was born, one paper by David Mathisen, an unknown but Sibylline physicist, delivered my physicist to his mission. That the world could be lost was not new but to frame time with that supposition, to give it dates as Mathisen had done, led him to think that he could interact with the process of human eschatology. And so he escaped the Rapturist's delusion that The Catastrophe cannot be avoided. He framed the experiment of a saved world.

After Dinner Speaker

> *We are in the Carinthia Lounge, a lounge named after a ship long scrapped but famous for the sailors' strike caused by passengers complaining that deckhands played skiffle music in their off hours.*

When he takes on others making the crossing
through this treeless passage,
when he conjures the concept of artificial leaves,
the others think his anaphora is anathema.
I cower. He does not:

    'The artificial leaf   is   one more source of fuel
    The artificial leaf   is   a metaphor for the real leaf
    The artificial leaf   is   developed by the scientific method*
    The artificial leaf   is   less complicated than the real leaf

*thus cutting short
    the half billion years nature took
        using CO_2 and sunlight
            to perfect a breath-enabling growth fuel.'

Give that man a ukelele.

The Patroniser

I cannot watch the dire
Sir Dogrel Olkincole,
or some such, shake his fist,
urge the dress suits and lace
                    to beware scientists.

'The artificial leaf produces ethanol, are you saying?'
'The artificial leaf can't produce pure alcohol yet but, yes…'
'Want to get drunk on your own roof, eh? Moonshine!'

      Sir Olkincole's sweet wife
pats my hand and murmurs,
    "Never mind. He doesn't
              really mean it. Really."

Genia in Memoriam:
Irène Joliot-Curie, Ida Noddack, Lisa Meitner

The first person to suggest that the nucleus of an atom could split in two parts and two of the leading experts in the analysis of the resulting debris were women.

Irony 1: Gender Fission

you could say the Great Bomb was delayed
by men who couldn't sit
with women first explaining
how an atom splits

Irony 2: The History of the Waist by Lisa Meitner
    Who Famously Described the Splitting Atom as Waisted

A man does not have a waist.
He has a midriff. A middle.
He also has a belly and a breadbasket,
a paunch, pot and general girth.

A woman has a waist.
A woman has been required to identify her waist.
A woman gains a neutron to do this.
A man remains a spherical uranium nucleus.

A woman has been deemed
beautiful in the absence of
a deep breath,
but a woman becomes
explosive when a waist of
energy is imposed upon her. She splits.

Irony 3: I Gain Confidence in the Ocean Metaphor
    Dominating This Book

Lisa Meitner
pictured
a nuclear explosion
as a drop
of water breaking

a simile of sea
volatile wet land

and her image of this invisibly small break
unlike Tennyson's whole grand sea
breaking, breaking,
breaking on its cold grey stones...

Irony 4
...inspired Enrico Fermi,
the unwaisted physicist,
to split the atom in Chicago
under a squash court.

No Irony Here
                      Noddack and Meitner, your comments please:

Being wasted researchers,
when we surmised what would happen
when the atom split,
we didn't suppose we would get the Nobel Prize
and we didn't.

I did.   *(Irène J-C)*
My name, maybe?

The Ghost of Marie Curie Works Up a Chorus While Chatting to Enthusiasts at a Model Engine Rally in 2015

All you men crouching by a nine-carriage train
that's stopped sauntering through the countryside, I know
you dream that what you've made will move again.
I know why you stay stooping

over cream and maroon livery when stock
rolls out of Gorpeton Blimey. You are checking
lost detail. You'll remake exactly what
you've made. Your trains are guarding,

circling, what was engineered long since. For once,
turn away from Bassett-Lowke traction engines,
read this ad for radium – *Buy a Piece*
Through the Post! Experiment!

Model Engineering knew in 1910
a woman had found what none of us could have made.
When I identified rays
that move through fog, through flesh, through fact, after

I'd ground, dissolved, collected precipitate,
I stunned a moment. Steam,
with its air of work and modernity – lost.
Oh, you've reconstructed my front-line X-ray cars!

They were nicknamed *les petites Curies*. They drove
away old views: perfect toys for discovering
the location of shrapnel
in bodies (broken, but they moved again.)

The Crystallier:
A Memoir in Which I Fable the Sociopolitical Side of Science

And in that disused lifeboat, the gods held a party.
Living saints attended.

At this rave, the God of Poetry, Brigid,
tripped over the snoozing God of Physics, Electron,

and begged him to deal with his boredom
since bosons are not trash.

The music of the spheres still taxed her.
So Electron lied: 'OK, right, I'm on it.'

Before drifting off again, he nudged my physicist
who, at that moment, was asleep himself

sagging over a table in the library at CERN
after a long shift attending the accelerator

and he woke from his weird dream of a rave
knowing that he must create a crystal for a low-energy future.

From decade to decade Brigid checked
that Electron had been on it

and Brigid gave credit to Electron's push of shy crystal researcher
into righteous deliverer of properly resourced outcomes.

Thus was my physicist received with joy in a few desolate marinas.
Brigid agreed with that good-time god, Electron,

that there should be a lyric outcome.
not for immortality, which the gods already have,

(electrons don't die ever)
but for mortals whom the gods seem to want to impress at parties.

Thus in the final tired hours of our world-saver voyage
I relax for an hour or two and dream of a Crystallier

> *and of Brigid*
> *who will transcribe this history*
> *into the Collection Celestial.*

On Not Being a Fish Given the Sea's Proximity

Back in the cabin, for a hard dance of work,
he calls on me, a non-scientist, to think.

I move my computer to our balcony
with its two plastic chairs and no windows.

Rainy wind on the muscular arm of rail.
He says, 'Metaphors are equations:

each side of the equals sign   is   an image that coincides
with one on the other side   and the whole phenomenon inheres
                        one truth   or two

$$E = hf$$
$$E \quad = \quad hf$$

    this describes the nature of sunlight as billions of photons

and of the digital camera
and of the mobile phone
and of the silicon chip
and of the computer
and of the e-book

and of the solar cell.'

And, after perhaps an hour, thinking of pagan marriage at sea, I
force out this thought:
                'w**E** are the same as the **h**and**f**asted.'

Marriage, a Sunbeat

Don't we feel the natural sound of sun
      beating inside itself as any human body beats?

Don't our atoms measure disruption
      into unexpected lines or graphs as we float on?

Do we take ourselves to heart and resonate?
      Are we all Antarctic ice sheets cracking

in weakening heat, singing under strain?
      Surely the sun gives us our physic.

Cabin Coffin

This is a bosun's game: imagine a ship foundering on an unexpected rock. In this catastrophe, one cabin of the hundreds on board, presumably a below water line cabin, is sealed off and two passengers perish in it –
Cabin Coffin.

Prayer Before Embarkation
(I devised this months before setting off
and recite it silently on the gangplank.)

To any God of any Human:
Bless the ship that we sail on.
If we drown before we arrive,
we pray to you our work to save.

I see the smile disappear from my physicist's face. Here, in this rising water, we are a society of twin souls, physicist and poet, a very special category in Cabin Coffin's soul-searching game. Passengers have no idea they have been chosen as contestants. Well, we know now. The brine inside our door is like a meat-eater's breath dangling its sinews over our vegetarian hands.

Yet there is a gold burnishing the diminishing room: is it the thing we've grasped that is almost in the world's grasp? Has it steamed off the physicist in his last fear, like last words? Or off me, like a poem, all lyric glitter bubbling?

So we are the Crystalliers and this is Cabin Coffin. The *S.S. Eschatology's* awarding body – there will surely be an award – will make an irritable statement that their awardees offer more than merely not to be. Their council will cite my physicist's passion. They will say – He Showed Us the Human Face of Science.
Which is now under water

They will say, he taught us this: wisdom is deciding between good and bad data. But there. Now I'm underwater myself. And in swims *Sorry*.

Aquarius

Our state room is polyphonic with *Sorry*
since experiments and poems
have not yet cooled the warming world.

      I tell him:
'You are balancing buckets –

your shoulders carry the burden of two poles:
      nurturing sun
      damaging sun.

      I see you
studying deserts,

divining light like water,
      freeing it for us,
      called to sense the sands…

      And then, Aquarius,
you'll save our age from us.'

Clifftop Meeting, a Flashback
The Needles, Isle of Wight

I fell by cloud. The greys of sky were wool,
were stitches, millions of them, and they spooled
out birds and unseen fishes and the whole
what-have-you of control.

I breathed that stuff as I fell through the air,
into my nose and throat, lanolin and hair,
till my inside was purled and plained and scared.
Who will care

that like a filament of yarn, I spun,
was whirled, unfurled, and hung on needle bones.
Dive, I did, I dived and did I land
on ground-sun coloured sand?

Think Workers

       The ship of our time is no tree
with a yard arm, a mast. No walnut shell rocks us home.

       Planes charge across skies, leaves blowing
away from the branch. But we two travel water-earthed

in this swaying skyscraper of a carbon-saver.

       We think
       We think and talk
       We talk of thoughts
                    We – what workers are this we –
                    think – what work is not thought –

       Whose thought crosses:
       hours with days
       power with energy
       means with ends

Electricity Generation in Germany in a Typical April Week

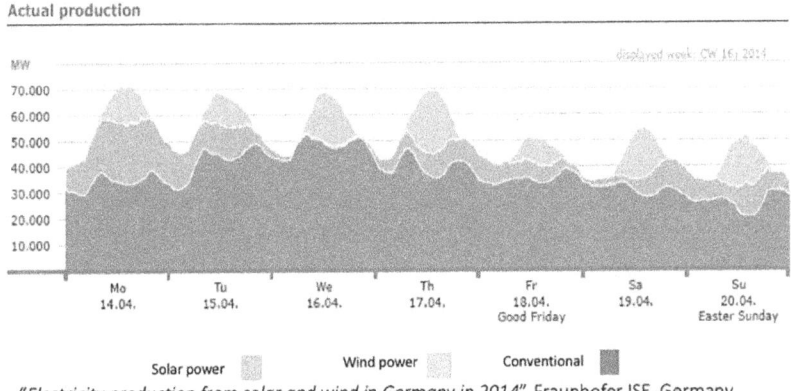

"Electricity production from solar and wind in Germany in 2014", Fraunhofer ISE, Germany

…while others say the sun doesn't shine enough,
it does.

        It shines most powerfully

at the peak of our demand,
when we most need it –

        the golden areas are small
        but they peak

        and peak
        when we most need them.

Gold Standard

    Outside, a feral surface.

        It hisses apart for our ship   seething and soothing

            the dry soles
  that walk our way.

      One of us
                meditates

    on how to demonstrate linkage

            repeatableconsistentreproducedoverandover.

The same one of us remarks on the glory of coincidence:

'Is sun gold
because, of all its photons,
golden ones
are the most plentiful?
Causal connection
or coincidence?'

'Coincidentally,
the energy of a golden photon
is just right for a solar cell
to operate most efficiently.'

                      No transcript of my response to this.

Surprise Kiss

Dolphins leap
out of the black-tipped waves
fins airstruck
up
drop
back to the still-filled sea.

Beyond our mahogany rail, porpoises –
on deck seven people are guessing 'Porpoises!' –
leap in their pairs and
black
shines, every colour.

In the shade of a lifeboat –
Quick!
Kiss!

and each synecdoche gives up its part.
                                        Since his arms clutch me in
                                        love, he has me now.

Since his arms clutch me in
fear and he pushes my mouth so
explosively in that salty air, a syll-
able enjambed, half fall-

ing
to a lower line, toss-
ing up the word that works for it-
self, love, and since that
has dis-
lodged my innate amorality and, though
force from anyone else would not show
love, he has me now.

A PAIR OF THREE

for Jude Barnham 1942–1994

The Visitor

While he was out I read a book.
I had to rest that day.
Then I heard a key in the lock
and steps in the hallway.

How could there be somebody there?
Yet listen: rustling bags,
clinking cup and running tap,
the snap of the kettle's plug.

Someone in her own place
settled with her tea.
Someone opened an old book
and sat relaxed like me.

I heard humming through the house
and skipping up the stair
yet when I held out my hand
I touched nothing there.

Later we sat down to eat
and talked about the day.
He shared difficult things but I…
I thought but couldn't say.

The Physics of Coincidence

      The red carriage

of fuchsia swung its bells to his foot falling
      towards my step.
His arm winged out to a parked car. My curls swung.
      If two atoms

share an electron and bond in one body
      in one compass-
ion of matter swaying with so much co-
      incidence direct-

ionless as the atoms that long for time
      to herd its lengths
into shocks that rope and weave each to each…
      then there's no which.

Mussels at Fisherman's Wharf, San Francisco Bay

in memory of Gerson Goldhaber

If I had asked Gerson what he knew
while we watched the sun's weight flatten Alcatraz –
if I had said: Have you physicists
observed the recognition these creatures feel
for the rocks they cling to ... But I asked:
What's your specialism? What is it you do?

So he outlined his job: to research the end
of the universe. To ask whether
our matter will continue to expand
as unlike a finish as one could hope.
Or will the world shrink? His graphs showed expansion.

While Keith dreams of sun and her, I dream
dark matter can stream memories from tachyons
that glow and flow to and fro in soul physics.

We parted in the dark. Look, iridescence
hasps wave-washed rocks clasped by salt water.
Though I'm freshwater – *unionida* – yet
Keith stayed rapt and homesick by the bay.

Those Keys

I am locked out.
He knows he has forgotten something.
Listen to him check, hose,
his secateurs?

Lavender sprays swathe
the long infirm necks and plush-red crowns
of bergamot.
How come odd old

plants have been let
to wane: skinny verbena, mauve sage?
Now I am left,
as we must each be left,

that bad thing I
would not face – I
have to think about it.
I'll kneel to think, I'll pluck back thick stalks

crowding a fennel thread.
The street light streams
its orange like hemerocallis
and wet soil shines.

Two mice eyes glint.
Fox rat death lurk.
He clutches the cold keys while he hums:
'Where has she gone?'

I Ask These Questions on a Country Walk

I'm no country person
I don't know
why

fern ochres will unfurl arteries

why

sorrel seeds will rash red

why

a beck will froth-crook over rocks

why

ranked crosswort will fiddle with air while either side of the
        stream green weed will strip trails of tree bones

why

grey fence will veil the lane

why

that stone will shroud with moss butterbur and ox-eye daisies

why

this field will spurt wild blood
    will be blood meadow

The Us

I ran downstairs
and said 'I've just thought:
We are random.
The you and I.
The she and you.
The she and I.
The us.'

'Here,' Keith said –
    he pushed aside his coffee,
        picked up the stapler he'd been using to hold together
        his notes on this and that background to this
        or that experiment –
'Here is a set of steel links'
    pointing to a line of staples.

I felt I was the wall
the molecules of his ordering thought
bounced against.

'And here' he said 'are the staples coming and going
gripping each other
and going
until…'

'No' I said and ran into the kitchen.
'Too many meanings!
Food is staples.
Look: are eggs random?'

'Oh I'm going to work on a paper,' he said,

and passing me as I stood by the fridge:
'Random interactions of molecules
led to increasingly complex molecules.
They became more and more complex
until they could start to replicate.'

And he hardly stopped at the door to say:
'Order in the universe increased tremendously
until love became an evolutionary principle.'

I ran upstairs.

We Shine Love So Hard

that we exchange our selves
in our day's reflections.
We wear each other's jacket
of worry. We walk thoughtfully

when there's a sudden onset
of mist. We place our soles
away from the skew of camber.
Careful. I can't see what will

betray your step. Or what will slip
under mine. Sometimes
the fog seems so much like
a mortal illness

that I hear: *Non lasciarmi –
don't leave me* – and hear
you murmur: *Ecco eccomi.*

Illyria by Rail

Evening: fur-
ragged sky bagging trees,
leaves dragging over pools stroked out of hiding

under ground.
Cosy up to strangers
while they listen to grandchildren, reading

Tripli-Cat
and Cat-Alogue, asking:
'The tooth fairy's note…was it in Mum's writing?'

They reply.
Point: 'Sea birds have arrived.
If there's a party in a field they're coming.

See that hedge?
The wrens hide there..' They say:
'What you know is what you choose to believe.' Turn

tightworded
away. Must we all leave
down the line lyrical lying where we will?

Moving On —

I was half-listening to the night
sounds of cars – on crises –
on essential works –

Reader – they slid me out of fear
to our car (unmendable –
so says the garage

church of free movement – but it goes)
Reader, you can't see our car –
you've seen your hand on

your own driver's door – your aches sink
to your stains as you read –
an owl taunted us –

who who who who who is driving
away at three a.m. –
driving toward what

the work is –

Overheard

*There's some disintegration you haven't done
that drapes the look of naked over bone.*

There's some disintegration you haven't done.
You're flesh. Since mine has gone
I am only bone.
Can we discuss the absence of eye and brain
in seeing and knowing you? No skeleton
should be alone.
May we sit here a moment?
An old bowl in the sun.
Nakedness fits us all so don't
insist on more than a memory of skin.
I have lost my bare surface. I've had to learn
to drape the look of naked over bone.

Heaven Is Nothing If Not Resolution

       Now we are over, death
has nuanced our model of dead worlds.
Indeed, as some poet mentioned,
pearl is mere pavement here
       and no one dead mourns.

His first wife shakes her head:
       'You worriers. You pair!'
       How death grated.
       How slow we were
       to greet it as family.

She swirls through souls to find us:
       New Wife Judicious.
Our titles shatter and no longer matter.
       Husband Clarified.
Doesn't a song have trouble ending lines?

If tachyons of energy connected us
       held us like hands
       whirling in trinity
       laughing at finity –
'Us warriors of loss. Us!' –

then his lost wife never was distressed
nor was she ever calling her widower.
       So a buried heaven
       has grown us in its glove –
now, here in this herbery, let's love.

REAL LEAR

You must bear with me. Pray you now,
forget and forgive. I am old and foolish.

The Tragedy of King Lear Act 4 scene 6

Lady Lear Dreams, Half-Wakes and Can't Remember

Flush of new flesh hardly there on my breasts and my back
Dresses flew up the bare aisle to an altar and nestled
Folly proposed to the A road 'Alight This is Home'
When? When was that?

Bird in the kitchen could not cheepcheepcheep and it shivered
Lentils and beans took an epoch to soften and render
Chutney sobbed glupglupglup glupglupglup glup on the Aga
Where? Where was that?

Subsequent houses loudpartied on subsequent nights
Dancer coughed into my palm as though my hand was his
Child in a rocking-horse cottage cried out and was silent
Who? Was she me?

Children would unhinge the sun when they pointed. Don't look
Green snowstruck lay like the body of god balmed with flakes
Sodden grass trodden
Why? Was it marked? With whose feet?

Backlane meandered me home like a hedgehog or vole
Carriage house shrank in its stone to a black fainting couch
Vicar escaped when a cat cracked its spine
Was I there?

Winter trees outstripped the briary fanged and ungardened
Roadside bumpbumped bumpbumpbumped along rut-runnelled field
Kerb kept a goshawk and harboured those car-deranged claws
What was it I wanted?

Chairs in a circle wake-waiting for silence to speak
Graveyard upraised each tumescence of earth
I thought that beyond me was nothing but soil
Who asked what it was that I feared?

Poornothing was mine
Did that civic that confine that parish enclose me
I don't say that girl who watched then was not me
But what then?

Those Corybant girls that I've hidden in ask
ask and turn.

Is Stepping Out Dying or Being Born?

the eau de nil leaves of the curling willow try
            during every rainfall
                        to go out from inside

the stem that holds their feet – they pierce a small door – this
            is how a shy one leaves
                        she wills a frail self – go

on the curve of the stem rain and sun unlock each
            wrapped-up leaf – I step out…

A Covert Bird

Out, I walk miles through fields to find the quail where it calls
its doubled syllables: *where where   wit wit*
I've left my shy writer in our stone home. She's shackled.
She's a pinioned creature: *there there   sit sit*
Our stones clutch air with swollen thumbs. Sick of cracked tarmac,
cold and teary, I turn: *scare scare   quit quit*
Back, limp room to room. Which is she locked in? Fly, quail, flush
up from your obscure run: *where where   wit wit*

Lear Exhorts Her Pareidolian Neighbours

Clouds, show me kind.
I see a pattern:
so let patterns rip through our consciousness.

Be companions
and let us cry out
at the sighting of shape. No? Oh, meaning

even if found
is stripped away, whipped
by wind: bunching wisteria, cutting

fuchsia barbs.
Representatives
of random hedge huddle from storms … hips haws

damson elder …
and wind hurls branches
across hurtsole carpets of beechmast stars.

Plants bellow, snarl,
elbow their sisters.
At the wind's goad, their seeds fly out of sight

understanding
there's another place.
The zephyr calls, come, to our stiff tendrils.

I command leaves,
stalks: bend to better.
Hyacinth, tree peony, dry heather,

don't sit scowling
purple: gorse golds us all
in its holy-wake. See! You are neighbours.

Lear Sees Herself as Her Own Environment

i Sward In Suburbia

Map, have a heart. My home is in you.
You rivet the L-shape of Lightheart Green.

Map, have a heart. My home is in you.
My borderward greens clasp worn streets.
The walnut tree huddles in Halfheart Green
while a householder drives her wooden stakes
along Overlong. Small flowers spread
purple under fences, defenceless
fences. Who gives a bench should clean a bench.
Someone is pitching balls from the irritable tarmac.
Boots, be the happiest lurkers far
below a faux-leather brimmed hat.
You rivet hell-shaped Lightheart Green.

ii Cheap Street Leat

through the hoar of years I've glittered
a bit, coruscate…

through the hoar of years I've glittered…
dashing down this alley's centre…
flicking Settle's pavement drinkers…
cooling paddling children … I'd have
run continuously happy
if you … in your torn and out-grown
flats gold boots or silver sandals…
had stayed dry … for falls of feet
crowd my filaments … you call
my flecks of light and clarity
a bit coruscate…

iii Green Ceramic Stream

those DownFromLondoners glimpse hints of dogs:
bit grrrr

those DownFromLondoners glimpse hints of dogs
eddying out of me ... believe I breed
hounds to heel incomers to splash them to growl
as they tiptoe across Welshmill weir...

I saw one DFL lean over the town bridge
and stare into my green ceramic stream...
she invoked all curs of homesick water...

so I invoked them too: surface now...
slaver fearsomely ... drop by drop
by drop by drop liquesce...

bit grrrr

iv Circular Staircase Behind a Bolted Door

my iron flowers
come on up

my iron flowers
a song from Singers grown
to be glimpsed through

cracked in my curvings carolling
my hard marble treads

my Selwyn forest oak banister
could be ridden up and slidden down
were that allowed

I wind into the forehead of the museum
and here … balconic … I stop…

come on up

Hazards and Thrown Humans

Whatever material you might consist of:
I'm wood.
If I pillowed my top layer – material
having a skin,
beneath it electrons are going and coming –
I'd soften
my surface, my tegument, down my flights – past
these hard pillars
that turn me and twist me – I could become twill.
I could bolster
the humans thrown down me, they would not break.
Window,
you melt, you transition – your glass, glass can hold it,
a body,
glass can flush back across opened space as a body
is hurled,
the thrown human will raise your resistance. A flash
of glaze holds
and the flesh does not shatter. And you, iron fence:
you cry 'Hazard!!!'
to passers-by. Guard rail, you can stop them, humans.
Persist.
Don't deny your ideals are forged out of you, beaten:
you're fixed
at three feet, but, young pickets, you quiver, you judder,
you shudder,
you shake and you tremble – excited! You'll bolt past
a spine,
an upside-down head. Up you go. Then when bone
and dear blood
slam at you, they'll meet metal sky. Why so thoughtless,
sweet matter?

Humans will lob, fling and sling their own species away, catapult
sisters and brothers. Inertia is not so supine
as it's strong.
We must learn to desist, then, materials: matter
does mind.

Crash, I Said

There were hazards, as they say, there.
Hidden driveways. There's always random. You don't know
whether Schrödinger's cat will be alive or dead when

you open the box. You only
observe. Is this a diversion, the wrong route? Try
to decide just how your interaction with the cat

kills it. You don't kill it. Something
already dead was sauntering out of its drive
towards the road where I was happy theorising

oneness, unnecessariness
of closure. Perhaps I thought immortality.
Luckily the dead person didn't believe in that

and gave way, giving me my head
past the camera. It was that kind of road: not built
up but long inhabited, not broad but wide enough,

so its hazards didn't faze me.
I'll reoffend and sometimes not against the law
but against my own judgement. It is when unzoned worlds

look out for me, pull out the dead
from under my wheels, or just cats, I kill nothing
or can kill nothing, over and over. Oh, I see

just reader: count, of my three justs,
how many positive, how many negative.
On balance – live, die – vision isn't a simple thing.

Falling from the Surface of the World, *or* Lady Lear's Rescue

Where was the world?
Burly as it is,
it saw to ice creams
while he, small enough to be grabbed
before he was killed,
was stilled

by me against
his will – I held him.
Did the whole human
parent not hear his *won't* defy
my tidal *stop*? Why
was I

the one to see
him jump onto rocks
to drown? He was caught
in my arms. I left bystanding
the world, left it less
careless.

Ars Matria, Ars Filia

My mother, dying, saw me sad
and blind.

My mother, dying, saw me sad
and said, 'I apologise.' [I never have
said sorry.] She lay under one sheet, not
asleep: 'I said poets are mad. I was wrong
to say it.' Each grain of light and lack of light
hustled by her bed. The wise nurse frowned
from her panopticon. The best enjambment
dies on the sheet and is remaindered. So,
the maternal body is not
unbreakable. She calls us to her lines. They radiate
and blind.

Lady Lear in the Canon

heads are floating at every level of the staircase
and going down they give off light

heads are floating at every level of the staircase...
marble bronze sometimes with a shaven shoulder

carry on up you long bud-sprout stalk
of a kale runt torch ... you cabbagehead lit
by a candle on top ... your thick-packed leaves
hard-veined as winter ... a simple candelabra
to the canon in this stairwell crowded
with mythic action ... what does it matter who
landed the boat or fought off the invaders...
men host every floor ... you inbetween

and going down you give off light

A God in Ascent

*Slip off, old body, push down, pull away, ripe
for the disembody.*

Slip off, old body, push down, pull away, rip.

I've assented. Discharged. Some part
will groan into space…

I'm clicking through
my million variants of analysis and decision,
clearer for the detach.

The sky is asserting its blinds, now sun and now night.

Body, you've been roughened up by your journey.
Battered by atmospheres. You couldn't have gone further.

But this svelte self … is it disassembling or freeing up
for the disembody?

Panic of an Autocrat

The Autocrat Attacks His Castellation
Walls, you have been unmalleable.
Undo yourselves. Expose me.
Let all your curbs be cut. Get holing. Now. Expose

                                                                    me.

The Autocrat Realises His Rampart Has Let Him Down
I trusted you to hold holes. Of light!
So shower me with lamps
of absent lump. Sun, moon and stars, come in, expose

                                                                      me.

Fracture, you bricks, unmoor stones,
get out blank blocks – out! Out!
Show I'm not stuck or thick. Crack on, fall down. Expose

                                                                      me.

The Autocrat Demands Deification from His Tribe
Now! My shoulder springs a wing
and slings me to the glory hole.
I'm going to be an ex-fixé. Don't repose

                                                                      me,

I'm ready for more than this tight-suited space.
No pride of place
should cement possibilities. Push, push, un-pose

                                                                      me

till I am shucked clear out of keep,
defenestrated. I
must be ex-posed. Exposed.

                                                                      Me.

Lear's Inwit

The Report said nothing.

It saw the desk approach in measured strides, the desk came on and did not stop. Until a vast edge lipped it, like the sealine on that beach where the Report had lain for perhaps an hour. It had trembled on a promontory, a reddish rock with crumbling margins. There had been eddies of breeze through it. Flutters of pages. Fingers had stroked it, withdrawn, pulled a cross over its whole frontage with damp fingers. Sweat. How much sweat was a part of the Report, those hours of shredding linen, of soaking, of stamping, hanging and drying. The sea had reminisced over a state the Report could not, itself, remember.

The Report said nothing.

The sea withdrew. The Report supposed it had been withdrawn from the beach, carried somewhere. The Report had been incomplete then. It could not fully comprehend its own status. It heard more as the torn legs of winged insects were drawn into shape on its inner leaves. The Report grew from the outside in. It thought more. It crisscrossed its thoughts till they comprehended, it seemed, enough truth and all reason. In the end, it could conclude. That was a realisation light and stark as the ancient elm in winter under which the Report had been left in one incomplete version; excited, bubbling with reference, elegant (it was sure) in its repetitions. The black tracery of elm boughs was so striking that the Report's arguments inhabited it fully, every wrinkling finger and arm of it, every year of its grace, every moment of the Report's disgrace. After which, though the elm was far away, the Report knew its own existence was a loved shadow like a winter tree.

The Report said nothing.

At this moment, lying on the hard breast of a desk, the Report was bereft. Of its role, of its power. Its words were Times New Roman 12 point. Its size was A4. Its pages were deckle edged, rough cut, stressed. Its covers were buckram with an acrylic coating. There was glue inside its spine. A ribbon, sewn from the top of its spine, held a particular page. The Report had become aware of its physical nature once it was placed in an upright position on the desk of its maker. Then, in a kind of darkness, a drawer perhaps, it considered its physical parts. Or had that been a bag stowed on a shelf? Waiting. Till I am born, the Report thought. Its birth had to be borne and was. The journey was comfortable but abrupt. The Report was drawn from the darkness even as a door opened through which its bearer moved, its tall bearer through a high doorframe.

The Report said nothing.

It was tossed as if thoughtlessly but the Report could think for itself. Of course it could. It needed no one else now. It could speak for itself. It had the language writhing within it. It had the context. It was prepared. It would be loved by these new communities of formica and wood and steel even as its growth had been loved. And the quiet of the desk, the office, its own office, its official nature, all grew like the power of the silent words – because closed – inside it. The Report would say so much. Exactly so much. It knew there was more than itself, well, how could any report think it was the only report or the begetter of reports. It was, simply, a made thing, a limit of pages, a cut of words, a closable document. It knew all that.

The Report said nothing.

Nothing unknown. It thought, for the first time, that it could only say what had been said. It could only repeat. Elegantly, in that cursive, that sweep, that autumn leave of falling read pages. It could do only what it had been prepared for. But the Report was unsatisfied. It knew itself, how was that? It knew its end, how did it? It could imagine – who knew that? Thinking of that, there was a kind of breath in it. Yet its writer had gone. Had lain it down and gone. Its owner did not hear its breath. Because the Report heard an intake and output of breath.

It was somewhere in the centre of its pages, the breath pulled some pages, tightened some words, all of it meant more.

The Report said nothing.

The Report practised the rising intake the falling output. It was drunk with the sensation. The desk surface, so obdurate softened. The light was high and elsewhere grew. Perhaps it was midday. With an enormous effort the Report carried itself upward, till it stood. Covers slightly turned, edges balanced like a dancer on the green leather, ribbon trailing behind as if it had lost its place. It opened itself just a fraction and faced the door.

The Report said:

Word Hurt

Words
drill walls
along my street.

Jolt
my brain
hips, knees, skull, feet.

Pain
builds thought
to break it. Verbs

dig
the road
and bulldoze kerbs.

Would-
worlds lay
infinitives,

make
tarmac
who-sensitive,

pierce
my gate,
gouge my flagstones.

Mind
has tools
and mends alone.

Virtual Memory in Dark Matter

You're looking for a past foothold
and I'm imagining: you
      gathering mint
      among lavender bushes
      looking for me. See me now?

Look. There's a red finger of cloud
pointing to Heaven's Valley.
      This yellow sky
      has undone it. See me now?
      Feelings stronger now? Stranger?

Though I know you're imagining
me here, I think in clichés:
      cracked glass heart, silk
      scarf in the back of a drawer.
      I don't see you. See me now?

Are you even aware that I'm imagining
you being aware? Someone
      dead is aware of me.
      See me now?
      See me now.

Like a Wasp Crawls On

a pane of air I'm
withheld my lungs lose
their breath I let my
distress undo you
unhold me your arms
withhold my shy off-
ice opens its tight
word hoard not one re-
liable you're warm
with holding me I
feel such shiver when
we are held we fly

Supplication in December

Oak hulk, will you
raise me?
How sturdily
you bear your tree-surgeon
swinging his workmighty arms and waistful of honed knives.

Full of honed knives
angling
sawing axing
filing cutting knadding,
a scimitarean woodman hacks hard, hacks high bones.

Hard hacks, high bones.
Your limbs
in his grinder
are being composted
under the bird-drained blue-proof sky till cut work is done.

Cut work is done.
Can you
stretch your clipped arms
to my leaf-stark rack-breath
bone-cart? Can you raise me in your hurt boughs through winter?

Gabbery

dry in the hedgeskips
a dunnock sings to her nestling
shatter shatter stalls the rain

I can see a never-dry
in peach curl and grey mould
in the yellow-spotted leaf
while I mop the muck sludge

every dry battletwig
scuttles under tubbans
a dunnock in the hedgeskips
sings to her nestling:

cuculus cuculus
gowk in my hidland
gabbery in my hidland
o fierce cuculus

gabbery: jest   hidland: secret place   cuculus,
gowk: cuckoo   battletwig: earwig   tubban: clod

Last Supper

The messes contract on my oak table. In the swill
of left red wine are flecks: fungus flies.
They drown or climb up the bowl
of my glass, crawling
like weevils.

Everything in my dining room grows small. The expense
does not. A thumbnail shell of date cake,
a thumb-sized swirl of hummus,
an eye-sized pancake.
All food squeezed

by hand: a grape slice is a green breast bared on velouté
of stringless celery. In that thin cream
my fork can't find its kicks.
Not on the speckled
porcelain.

Nor in the half-poached egg topped by a red-ribbed new-born leaf.
Not in fish slush mash. Why does the chef
not show himself while I shrink
from aerobatic
bugs amok

above my three pieces of cheese – micro, mini, palm-fit –
tied down and draped with tired chives.
They melt. Then, fruitlessly,
flies close on my mouth,
plain and sour,

hunting a digestif … not fruitless … at last I find where
the shy chef hides: inside the dessert,
among cacao fragments. Tastes
I can't identify
bite, nip, sting.

Soundsunder

I'm used to sitting without speaking
to others
sitting by me without speaking

till one of us says: it's time to talk
to others
beside yourself and time to break

up silence all together   Alto-
gether we
chat and chatter and all without

the noise I hear without speaking
before we
begin to talk our lip and trip

of sound   Ear isn't empty nor without
its other
world   I hear inside my silence

that it is the sussuround of us
we other:
sounds that shushhush the our of self

www.ingramcontent.com/pod-product-compliance
Lightning Source LLC
Chambersburg PA
CBHW031633160426
43196CB00006B/394